JUNIOR

First Facts

The Wild WEST

Written by Antony Mason
Illustrated by Malcolm Stokes

HENDERSON
PUBLISHING PLC

©1994 HENDERSON PUBLISHING PLC

High noon in Frontier Town

The door to the saloon bar squeaked on its hinges in the dry desert wind. Otherwise all was quiet in Frontier Town - dead quiet - as two men walked slowly towards each other down the dusty street. Frightened townsfolk peered out from their windows. Jesse and Billy had begun arguing in the bar. Now they had decided to settle their argument with guns.

Jesse looked at Billy, waiting for him to make the first move. His hand hovered nervously over the Colt revolver in his holster. Salty sweat dripped from under his cowboy hat into his eyes. He knew Billy was quick on the draw - very quick.

THE WILD WEST

Suddenly two horsemen burst into the street, riding at speed. One of them wore a star-shaped sheriff's badge which flashed in the bright sunlight.

"The game's over, boys," he shouted. "Draw your guns and you are both dead men! Indians are attacking the Browns' ranch and we need all the guns and riders we can get. Saddle your horses and follow me!"

It was just another day in the Wild West. Or was it? This the picture of the Wild West painted by films and books.
But what was it really like? In this book we are going to find out.

THE WILD WEST

Indian lands

The Wild West covered a vast area in the middle of the USA. People only began to call these lands the Wild West about 150 years ago, when cowboys, farmers, gold miners and outlaws began to move into it.

Before then, just about the only people living in these regions were Indians. They had been living here for thousands of years. Some of them were hunters, always on the move in search of game and fish; others were farmers, who lived in small villages and grew crops in the river valleys.

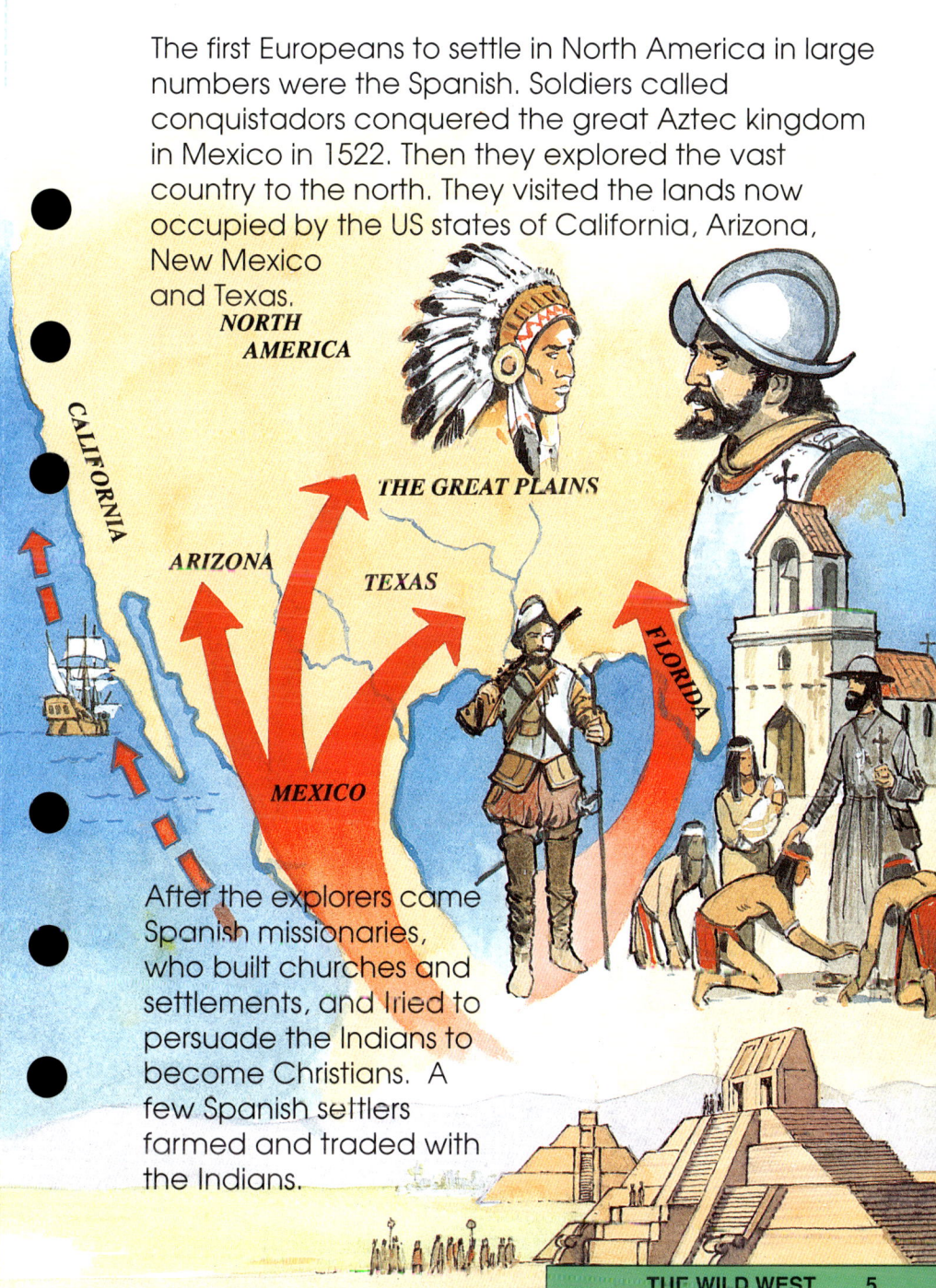

The first Europeans to settle in North America in large numbers were the Spanish. Soldiers called conquistadors conquered the great Aztec kingdom in Mexico in 1522. Then they explored the vast country to the north. They visited the lands now occupied by the US states of California, Arizona, New Mexico and Texas.

After the explorers came Spanish missionaries, who built churches and settlements, and tried to persuade the Indians to become Christians. A few Spanish settlers farmed and traded with the Indians.

THE WILD WEST 5

The arrival of the horse

The Spanish brought horses with them. It was the first time people in North America had seen horses. At first they were frightened of them. But soon the Indians found they could also ride them - and ride them extremely well.

Horses changed the lives of the Indians of the Great Plains of North America, such as the Sioux, Cheyenne, Comanche and Blackfoot. They used them to hunt the vast herds of buffalo that roamed the grasslands of the Plains.

The Indians of the Great Plains travelled about the land with their horses, following the herds of buffalo. They took with them their leather tents, called tepees, and set up camp wherever they needed to stop and hunt. Men, women and children all had their jobs to do around the camp.

Sometimes they would turn their spears, bows and arrows, and tomahawks against other Indian tribes, and go to war. But generally they were peaceful: there was always plenty of food, because there were so many buffalo to hunt - as well as other animals such as deer and hares.

THE WILD WEST 7

Indian ways of life

There were many different Indian tribes in America. The way that they lived depended on the kind of country that surrounded them. The Hopi and other Pueblo Indians lived in the dry, rocky regions of Arizona and California. They built large villages out of mud bricks on the cliff tops, or in caverns in the cliffs, where they could be safe from their enemies. They grew sweetcorn, and made beautiful baskets and pottery.

8 THE WILD WEST

There were numerous tribes living in the Rocky Mountains, which stretch all the way down the western side of North America. They included the Paiute, Flathead and the Nez Percé. They lived by hunting and fishing, and gathering fruits and berries. They trapped animals for food, and also to make fur clothes to keep them warm in winter.

THE WILD WEST

Discovering the West

During the 18th century the USA became an independent country, and it was fast becoming a rich nation. But all the towns, cities and industries were on the east coast. In 1803 the USA bought from the French a huge area of land in the middle of North America. It was called Louisiana, named after the French king, Louis XIV.

Suddenly the Americans realised that they knew very little about the vast land that lay to the west of them.

10   THE WILD WEST

The Americans decided that they needed to know more about their own country. In 1803 Captain Meriwether Lewis and Captain William Clark led an expedition right across the continent to the west coast. They were often helped by the Indians, such as the Shoshoni and Chinook, but had to fight against the Blackfoot. They returned in triumph after over two years: it was the first time a European expedition had crossed America.

THE WILD WEST 11

Mountain men and wagon trains

Lewis and Clark had discovered what a huge and rich country lay across the Great Plains, the Rockies and the lands of the west coast. Soon a few adventurous people began to head west, to see what they could find.

The first were trappers. In those days, furs were very valuable, and trappers found they could make a living by travelling all the way to the Rockies to trap beavers, raccoons and other fur animals. These 'mountain men', as they were called, met the Indians. They often worked with them, and sometimes fought with them. Some of them had Indian wives.

Gradually many Americans began to realise that they too could make a living by travelling west to find new lands to farm. They were often poor people, who sold everything they owned to make the journey. Whole families would travel together in a group of wagons pulled by oxen, called a wagon train. They had to take with them everything they needed for the journey and their new life in the West.

These 'pioneers' followed trails across the Rockies, such as the Oregon Trail, often helped by mountain men and Indian guides. When they arrived in the West, they lived in very simple log cabins and farmed the land around them.

THE WILD WEST

Forts

Some Indians accepted the pioneers. Others wanted them to pay for crossing their lands. And some were worried that the newcomers would take their land.
There were misunderstandings, and arguments flared up. Sometimes the Indians attacked and killed the pioneers, and stole their possessions. The pioneers needed to be armed with guns. To protect themselves at night they would put the wagons in a circle, called a corral, to make a kind of fort.

There were trading posts along the trails, where the pioneers could stop and rest on their six-month journey. Indians would come to these trading posts to exchange furs and food for blankets, guns, ponies, tobacco and whisky.

The trading posts were often built like fortresses, to protect the warehouses, and also to protect travellers and traders from attacks by Indians. Many trading posts also had small army detachments.

These were lawless lands, already ruled by the power of the gun.

THE WILD WEST 15

California, here I come!

Meanwhile, Mexico was becoming worried that America wanted to take over its lands, which at that time included Texas, New Mexico, Arizona and California. In 1836 Davy Crockett and other settlers were killed by the Mexican army at a mission station in Texas called the Alamo. By 1845 the USA was fighting a full-scale war with the Mexicans. After three years the USA won, and took over all these territories from Mexico.

In 1848 gold was discovered in the wild hills and rivers of California. Suddenly thousands of settlers flooded across America on the trails to look for gold. This was called the Gold Rush, and many people made a fortune. Many of them lost it again, and many had no luck at all. The gold also attracted all kinds of ruffians, tricksters and thieves, who wanted to get rich quickly, by whatever means they could.

In just a few years San Francisco grew from a village into a bustling town.

THE WILD WEST 17

The Railroads

Between San Francisco and the cities of the east coast of the USA lay thousands of miles of open country. It was a long, slow journey by wagon train. In 1858 stage-coach services began carrying mail, money and passengers in fast, horsedrawn carriages. They took just 25 days to cross America. The most famous stage-coach company was called Wells Fargo.

Because the stage coaches carried money, they were often attacked by bandits, as well as by Indians.

Meanwhile, bit by bit, railways were built across the USA, gradually connecting the east coast cities to the new farmlands of the Midwest states, such as Kansas, Nebraska and the Dakotas.

- Stations at the end of these railway lines became cattle markets. Cattle were raised across huge areas of open grassland in the central part of the country, especially in Texas. To begin with, these cattle were longhorns, which were almost wild. Each year they would be rounded up and taken to be sold at the cattle towns on the railways.

- The men who rounded up the cattle were called cowboys.

THE WILD WEST 19

The Cowboys

It was a rough, tough life being a cowboy. Cowboys spent almost all day riding their horses, driving thousands of half-wild cattle over rocky trails and through rivers. They camped out under the stars, and cooked their meals over open fires.

Cowboys had their own kind of uniform. They wore tough, high-heeled riding boots with spurs attached; thick leather chaps to protect their legs from thistles and cattle horns; neck-scarves which they could put over their mouths to keep out the dust and flies; gloves to protect their hands; and broad-rimmed felt hats to keep the sun and rain off their heads.

20   THE WILD WEST

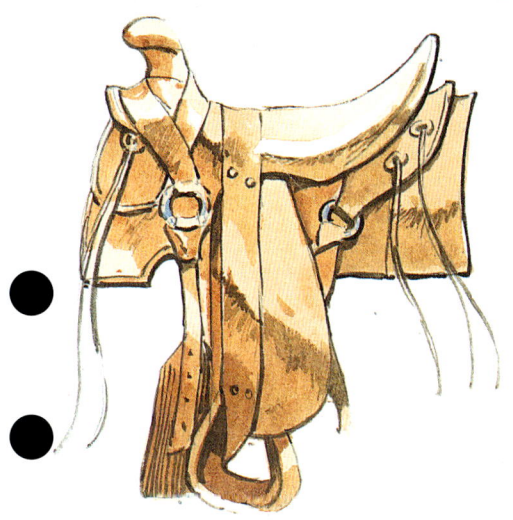

Cowboys had special saddles, called 'western saddles', which had a high pommel on the front. They could use this to help them in their work, for instance to hold a rope when they lassoed cattle.

When cowboys reached the cattle towns they received their payment - which was never very much. Many of them then spent it all there and then - on saddles and boots, guns and ammunition, and also on card games and drinking. Their wild behaviour often resulted in fights - sometimes gunfights. They also organised rodeos, in which they could show off their skills in riding wild horses, and roping calves.

After the 1880s cowboys began to work more and more on ranches, where tamer cattle were fenced in by barbed wire.

THE WILD WEST 21

A railway across America

In 1869 the Union Pacific Railway was opened. It went right across America to San Francisco, and now people on the east coast could travel to the west coast in a single journey. This was an extraordinary feat of engineering. Much of the building was done by labourers from China.

Thousands of settlers began to move towards the West. Small towns grew up all along the way, and more and more of the surrounding land was taken over for farming.

This was Indian land, and the Indians did not like it. They were being invaded from all sides, by the wagon trains, railways, new towns, cattle ranches, small farmers and gold diggers. Hunters arrived with powerful guns and killed buffalo in their thousands: within just a few years the buffalo herds had been almost wiped out.

The US government offered the Indians new areas of land, called reservations, where they could live and farm. But the land was often very poor, and many of these Indians were not farmers, but hunters.

The Indians saw that their whole way of life was under threat.

THE WILD WEST 23

Indian wars

At first there were arguments between settlers and the Indians; then there were fights; then there were battles. There were cruel massacres on both sides, when men, women and children were killed. The US government sent the army to protect the settlers and to punish the Indians. They made treaties with the Indians, but often broke their promises.

In 1876 Colonel Custer, leading the 7th US Cavalry, went into battle against the Sioux. The Sioux, led by Chief Crazy Horse, won a famous victory called the Battle of Little Big Horn, and Custer and all his men were killed.

After this the US army waged a fierce war against the Indians. Soon almost all the Indian tribes had been made to live in reservations.

In 1890 a strange craze developed among the Sioux. They held ceremonies called 'Ghost Dances'. The dancers said that their bodies could resist bullets. American settlers took fright and called in the army.

A group of Sioux surrendered to the 7th US Cavalry but were gunned down at a place called Wounded Knee Creek. This tragedy marked the end of the Indian Wars, and the final defeat of the Indians.

THE WILD WEST 25

Frontier towns

Throughout the history of the Wild West, small towns were built along the edge of the country that marked the frontier between land that was settled and farmed and the unknown Indian lands beyond.

They were rough places, usually little more than a high street of wooden shops and other buildings. Often they would only last a few years before another town was built further along, and the first would be abandoned.

Local farmers and their families would come to the frontier towns to sell their produce and to buy the things they needed. Many of these farmers had borrowed money from a bank to buy land, so banks were important.

Shops sold tools, seeds, cloth, needles, shoes, saddles, guns and ammunition, cooking pots, plates and bowls, coffee, flour, beans - everything a family might need.

The blacksmith was an important figure in these towns. He put shoes on horses, and made metal wheel rims and all kinds of tools.

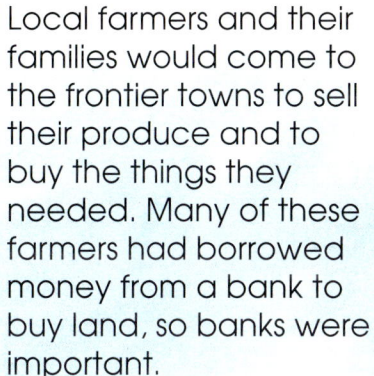

THE WILD WEST 27

The Good, the Bad and the Ugly

In a frontier town there would usually be a small church or chapel, a school, and, of course, a graveyard.

Larger towns would have hotels, where visiting salesmen, landowners, bankers and lawmen could stay, as well as richer settlers on their way west. Some of these hotels would put on shows, such as music-hall acts of singing and dancing.

The hotels also had bars or saloons, where people would come to drink, play cards and meet friends.

People often drank too much in the Wild West, and ended up having fights.

28 THE WILD WEST

Then the sheriff, or his deputy might be called in to sort out the problem, and perhaps make an arrest. There were a lot of wild people in the Wild West: rough cowboys, outlaws and criminals, drunkards and madmen. Many of them were quick to pull their guns and shoot if they got into an argument. The sheriff or marshal - the chief lawman - had to be a brave man if he wanted to keep order in his town.

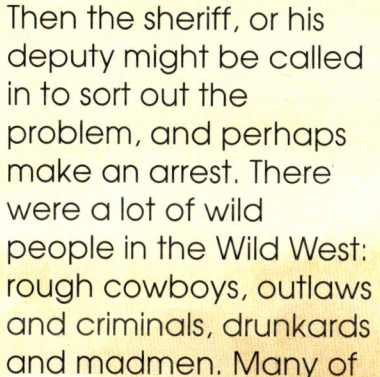

THE WILD WEST

Famous outlaws and law men

Some of these outlaws became famous throughout the Wild West, such as Jesse James, who was killed in 1882. Billy the Kid was an outlaw in New Mexico. He killed a number of his enemies, before being killed by Sheriff Pat Garrett in 1881.

Jesse James

Billy the Kid

The most courageous lawmen also became famous, such as Wild Bill Hickok, who, as Marshal, sorted out the railway town of Abilene. Wyatt Earp was a lawman in Wichita and Dodge City in the 1870s. In 1881 he had a famous gunfight at the OK Corral in Tombstone, Arizona.

Wild Bill Hickok

Not all the bandits were men. Belle Starr, the 'Bandit Queen' was a gang leader in the Wild West, until she was shot dead in 1889. Martha 'Calamity Jane' Cannery was a famous rough-and-tough cowgirl.

Belle Starr

Wyatt Earp

30   THE WILD WEST

The Wild West had become a legend even in its own time. Buffalo Bill Cody's Wild West Show, which began in 1883, travelled through much of the USA as well as Europe. It was a kind of circus starring all kinds of western acts, such as shooting, riding bucking broncos and lassoing.

Soon Hollywood was making the first Western films. The film industry even employed real bandits of the old Wild West. A bank robber called Emmett Dalton was shot and captured in Coffeyville, Kansas, in 1892. After he left prison in 1907 he wrote film scripts for the cinema, and made this his career until his death in 1937.

Western films were popular even before the Wild West had come to a close - and they have been popular ever since.

THE WILD WEST 31

Words about the Wild West

blacksmith a person who works with iron, using a hammer, an anvil and the intense heat of a forge.
buffalo a large, shaggy member of the cattle family, also called a bison. There used to be millions of buffalo on the Great Plains, but they were hunted almost to extinction in the late 19th century.
corral a circle of wagons drawn up for defence; also a fenced area of a ranch.
frontier town a town on a frontier or border. In the Wild West, these were rough, quickly built towns on the frontier between settled lands and Indian country.
lasso a noose made of rope and leather, used by cowboys to capture cattle, usually by throwing the noose over the animal's neck. Also called a lariat.
longhorn cattle a half-wild breed of cattle of the Great Plains. Their horns could be up to 1.5 metres across. They were later replaced by tamer breeds which produced more meat and were raised on ranches.
marshal a lawman, similar to a sheriff, appointed to keep order in a town or district.
missionary someone who travels to other lands to try to convert people to his or her religion. Christian missionaries tried to convert the Indians of the West.
mountain men American or Canadian trappers who lived among the Indians of the Rocky Mountains, especially from about 1805 to 1870.
pioneer anyone who is part of the first group of people to do something new. In the Wild West, the term was used for the first settlers, most of whom had travelled overland with the wagon trains.
pommel the large handle-shaped knob at the front of a western saddle.
reservation an area of land put aside by the US government for Indian tribes. Indians were often forced to live in reservations against their will.
saloon bar the name for any bar in a Wild West town, where alcoholic drinks, especially whisky, were sold.
settler a person who travels to a new land with the intention of staying there.
sheriff the chief lawman of a district. Sheriffs were usually elected officers.
tepee a triangular-shaped tent, made of wooden poles and leather, used especially by the Plains Indians.
tomahawk a fighting axe used by Indians.
outlaw a criminal who lives 'outside the law', and so cannot expect the protection of the lawmen.